We Can Stay Safe

WITHDRAWN

Rebecca Rissman

Heinemann Library
Chicago, Illinois

www.heinemannraintree.com
Visit our website to find out
more information about
Heinemann-Raintree books.

To order:
☎ Phone 888-454-2279
🖥 Visit www.heinemannraintree.com
to browse our catalog and order online.

Edited by Rebecca Rissman, Siân Smith, and Charlotte Guillain
Designed by Kimberly Miracle and Joanna Malivoire
Illustrated by Paula Knight
Originated by Capstone Global Library
Printed and bound in China by Leo Paper Products Ltd

14 13 12 11 10
10 9 8 7 6 5 4 3 2 1

Library of Congress Cataloging-in-Publication Data
Rissman, Rebecca.
  We can stay safe / Rebecca Rissman.
    p. cm.
  Includes bibliographical references and index.
  ISBN 978-1-4329-3337-1 (hbk.) -- ISBN 978-1-4329-3338-8
(pbk.) 1. Accidents--Prevention--Juvenile literature. 2. Youth-
-Health and hygiene--Juvenile literature. I. Title.
  HV675.5.R57 2008
  613.6--dc22
                        2008055662

Acknowledgments

We would like to thank Nancy Harris and Adriana Scalise for
their help in the preparation of this book.

Every effort has been made to contact copyright holders of
any material reproduced in this book. Any omissions will
be rectified in subsequent printings if notice is given to the
publisher.

Some words are shown in bold, **like this**. They are
explained in "Words to Know" on page 23.

Contents

Acting Safely 4

Fire Safety 8

Water Safety 10

Home Safety 12

Bicycle Safety 14

Road Safety 16

Your Own Safety 18

Asking for Help 22

Words to Know 23

Index 24

Note to Parents and Teachers 24

About this series

About this series: Books in the **Stay Safe!** Series introduce readers to simple but important safety tips. Use this book to stimulate discussion about how children can stay safe in a variety of situations.

Acting Safely

Everyone is special. Everyone should act safely.

Acting safely means being careful. Acting safely means not doing things that could hurt you. Acting safely means not doing things that could hurt others.

When we act safely, we ask for help when we need it.
When we act safely, we remember the rules.

Fire Safety

Fire is dangerous because it can burn you or make it hard to breathe. To stay safe, do not play with matches. Do not use a stove by yourself.

When we act safely, we look out for others. It is very important to look out for children who are younger than you.

If you see a fire, do not panic. If your clothes catch fire, always remember to stop, drop, and roll on the floor.

Water Safety

lifeguard

It can be fun to play in water. But it can also be dangerous. To stay safe in the water, always swim near a **trusted** adult, such as a **lifeguard**. Wear a **life jacket** or use floats if you need them.

To stay safe in boats or rafts, always wear a life jacket and sit still. Only go in boats when the weather is clear.

Home Safety

There may be dangerous things in your home.
To stay safe, do not touch things that are sharp.
Do not touch things that are hot.

To stay safe, do not play with pills or other medicines.
Do not play with electric **plugs**. Do not play on the
stairs because you could fall.

Bicycle Safety

It can be fun to ride bicycles. But it can also be dangerous. To stay safe, always wear a **helmet** and ride on a safe **path**.

To stay safe, do not ride a bicycle that is too big for you. Do not ride on busy roads.

Road Safety

Roads are busy places. Roads may be dangerous. To stay safe, never play by a road. Always find a safe place to play, such as a playground.

To stay safe, always look both ways and listen for traffic before you cross a road. If the road is very busy, use a tunnel or bridge to cross it.

Your Own Safety

Your safety is important. To stay safe, do not talk to **strangers**.

Do not accept gifts from strangers. Always say "No, thank you." Do not help strangers. You could tell a **trusted** adult if you see a stranger who needs help.

If you are out and you need help, look for a **trusted** adult, such as someone in a **uniform**. You might find a police officer to help you or someone else who can keep you safe.

Learn your address and phone number. If you feel lost, wait in a safe area and ask a trusted adult for help.

Asking for Help

Who Can You Ask for Help?

- ✓ Police Officer
- ✓ Cross walk attendant
- ✓ Teacher
- ✓ Doctor
- ✓ Nurse
- ✓ People in **uniform** who work in a **public place**, such as a supermarket or museum

Words to Know

helmet — special hard hat to protect your head

life jacket — jacket that helps you float and helps to keep you from going under the water

lifeguard — someone who works at a swimming pool or on a beach to help people who are in danger

path — area that is set aside for people away from traffic. A bike path is for people on bicycles.

plug — something that goes into an outlet to make a machine work

public place — place where people are allowed to go

stranger — person you do not know

trust — believe that something is right

uniform — set of clothes people have to wear for their job which makes them look the same. For example, police officers may all wear the same uniform so that people can tell who they are.

Index

bicycle 14, 15
fire 8, 9
helmet 14, 23
police officer 20, 22

public place 22, 23
lifeguard 10, 23
road 16, 17

stranger 18, 19, 23
trust 10, 19, 20, 21, 23

Note to Parents and Teachers

Before Reading:

Ask children if they know what acting safely means and if they can think of a time when they acted safely. Explain to children that being safe means being careful, staying out of danger, and not hurting yourself or others.

After Reading:

- Create a chart with children about people they can ask for help if they feel unsafe.
- Ask children to role-play staying safe with partners or in small groups. Children can make up their own skits or they can be assigned situations. Give them time to practice and ask them to show their performances to the class.
- If possible, ask the fire department to come and talk to children about fire safety.
- Brainstorm ways children can keep themselves safe. Give children a piece of paper so they can create their own sign entitled "Rules for Keeping Yourself Safe."